Scotch Whisky

Text by: Tom Bruce-Gardyne

Colin Baxter Photography, Grantown-on-Spey, Scotland

Scotch Whisky

Viewed from Space, Scotland is like a tiny, jagged fist on the eastern edge of the North Atlantic. The likeness is telling, for this small country with a population half that of London, punches well above its weight in terms of its influence on the world and its level of recognition. For millions, Scotland is a distant, mysterious place that they will never visit. They may have only the haziest idea of where it is and what goes on there, but they know its name, and they know it because of whisky.

Scotch is Scotland in a bottle. It is a distillation of its homeland that somehow manages to reflect a little of its bittersweet, melancholic beauty. For such a small country, the range of landscape is extraordinary, from the pastoral Lowlands to that great wilderness of the Highlands. You do not have to travel far for the view to change dramatically – from rolling farmland to sudden granite peaks or from a sheltered loch to the storm-tossed coast and the islands beyond. Something of this diversity is captured by every single distillery making malt whisky in Scotland.

Of course it was never a conscious decision to do this, it just happened that way. When Talisker began distilling on the Isle of Skye, it was only natural that the whisky should reflect its environment with the Cuillin mountains behind and the cold, grey Atlantic out front. It was a local whisky for local people. It had to be a full-bodied malt with a big, fiery heart to imbue warmth and well-being. Something gentle and understated would never have really caught on, on Skye.

There are similar stories for every one of the eighty or so malt whisky distilleries currently operating in Scotland. Each one produces a unique spirit out of the same humble recipe based on malted barley as their neighbour. As each single

Established in 1786, Strathisla (opposite) is one of the oldest distilleries in Scotland – its twin pagodas add an oriental note to the Speyside town of Keith.

Putting fire in the belly of Highland Park on Orkney – one of the few distilleries left that still malts its own barley.

When comparing single malts, or different expressions of the same malt, professional tasters like to use proper tasting glasses. These are small and tulip-shaped with clear glass. First the colour will be assessed for clues about maturity. Then it will be sniffed, first neat and then with a little water added, before it is finally tasted.

malt starts its slow journey to maturity, tiny differences in aroma and flavour begin to multiply over time to create something truly individual and precious in the glass.

The history of making whisky serves as a fascinating mirror to this sometimes troubled country. For centuries whisky, or at least good Highland whisky, was the very spirit of defiance. As Robbie Burns said 'whisky and freedom gang thegither (together)'. It was perfect for drinking as a toast to friendship and as a two fingered salute to those seeking to tame and control the land. Though we cannot know exactly what the original whisky tasted like, it would have been hot and rough compared to the mellow, well-matured spirit of today.

Whisky is obviously no longer made in illicit stills by smugglers in remote bothies. It is now a big and very important industry for Scotland and for the Government who tax it so heavily. Yet it still has a certain edge that demands respect with its grown-up taste. Even the smoothest dram is no crowd-pleaser on first acquaintance – and there's something very Scottish about that.

Malt or Blend?

There are two main types of Scotch whisky – 'Single Malts' and 'Blends'. The former has to be made in a pot still at a single distillery using water, malted barley and no other cereals. Blends are a mix of single malts and grain whisky, which is made in a continuous still. It is often said that malts were the original whisky, though whether they tasted much like modern day single malts is another matter. Blends took off under the Victorians and came to dominate whisky drinking, and today account for around nine out of ten bottles of Scotch sold. It is untrue to say that one is necessarily better than the other. Single malts tend to be older and more expensive, and while blends vary in quality, the finest can be made from up to thirty or forty well-matured malts. In addition to the above, there are three other official types of Scotch: 'Single Grain Scotch Whisky' made at a single distillery using a mix of malted barley and other grains. 'Blended Grain Scotch Whisky' – a blend of grain whiskies from various distilleries, and 'Blended Malt Scotch Whisky' – a blend of Single Malts such as Johnnie Walker Green Label.

A History of Scotch

No-one knows when the first drop of whisky was distilled in Scotland, but the first recorded mention was in the Exchequer Roll of 1494 when a monk in Fife was granted the right 'to make *aquavitae*'. This Latin word meaning 'the water of life' was translated into Gaelic as *uisge beatha* (pronounced 'oosh-key-ba') which became 'uiskie' and eventually 'whisky' in the early 18th century. Compared to today's whisky, it would have been a rough, fiery spirit made from whatever cereals were available, and drunk almost straight from the still. To make it more palatable it was sometimes sweetened with herbs, sugar or spices. The drink also had medicinal properties. It was used to rub on aching joints and as a surgical spirit for cleansing wounds.

The knowledge of distilling spread across the country and whisky-making developed as a local cottage industry to supply the home and those nearby. It took place on farms during the cold winter months after the harvest, whenever there was grain to spare. The one exception was Ferintosh, the country's oldest commercial distillery that was built near Dingwall on the Black Isle in the 1670's. It survived for just over a century by which time it was making two thirds of the legal whisky in Scotland. Its passing was lamented in a poem by Robbie Burns, who was a keen admirer of Ferintosh.

By the mid 18th century there were already a few big distilleries in the Lowlands who were part of the early Industrial Revolution and concerned with producing whisky on an ever increasing scale. There were also a great number of much smaller distillers operating outside the law. These could be found everywhere from the furthest flung corners of the Highlands to the centres of population. In Edinburgh at this time, it was claimed there were 400 stills bubbling away,

A whisky smuggler with his pot still somewhere on Speyside in the early twentieth century. Whisky smuggling had been rife in the region a century before, but most illicit distillers came in from the cold after the Excise Act of 1824.

THE CELEBRATED "BANTASKIN" AND "OLD SILENT" MALT LIQUEUR HIGHLAND WHISKIES.

TO BE HAD ONLY FROM B.⁺ MACKAY, QUEEN'S BUILDINGS, Lenzie. SCOTLAND.

Early advertising for Scotch whisky was never too subtle when it came to hammering home the national stereotype. In this 1902 poster with its kilts, bagpipes and misty lochs, only the shortbread tin appears to be missing.

odds were firmly in favour of the distillers, particularly those in the Highlands and Islands who had a vast wilderness to hide in.

There was also a growing thirst for the whisky which was produced in small stills at a slow pace, unlike the industrial spirit pumped out by the big distillers down south. For some drinkers, the fact it was illegal, made it taste all the sweeter. As an Irishman once said of his country's moonshine – poteen; it was 'superior in sweetness, salubriety and gusto to all that machinery, science and capital can produce in the legalized way.' Higher taxes on legitimate Scotch at the end of the 18th century only fuelled demand for its illegitimate cousin which was smuggled across the country along the old droving roads to cities like Dundee and Perth. Much of it was made on Speyside, particularly Glen Livet which became a one industry glen almost overnight, with around 200 stills hidden in remote crags and bothies. The fame of its whisky even reached King George IV

of which only eight were licensed.

Tax on drink and those who made it had been one of the main sources of revenue in Scotland since the Act of Union of 1707. With so much illicit hooch being made, the Government became increasingly desperate to reassert control and claw back its income by stamping out the whisky smugglers. For some time the who demanded some illicit Glen Livet the moment he stepped ashore in Edinburgh at the start of his State Visit of 1822. A year later the Government passed the Excise Act which meant distillers could obtain a license for just £10. Those who refused to comply were to be hunted down and punished. Most distilleries decided to come in from the cold including such famous names as Macallan, Glenlivet and Cardhu.

In 1830 an Excise officer in Dublin named Aeneas Coffee invented a new type of still that was to revolutionise the whisky industry. Because it worked continuously, it produced spirit in far greater volume than the old pot still, that could only make one batch at a time. Pot stills have always been used for making malt whisky while continuous stills are used for grain whisky. When the two were mixed together to make the first blended Scotch whisky, the Scots created a drink that would eventually conquer the world. Interestingly it could well have been Irish blends that blazed a trail with Scotch trailing in their wake. Coffee had originally offered his new invention to distillers in his native Ireland, but they turned him down.

Many of today's famous brands of blended Scotch were created by Victorian grocers, like the Chivas brothers in Aberdeen, the Walkers of Kilmarnock and Arthur Bell in Perth. They would buy casks of malt and grain whisky

A typical period advert from 1899 .

The Bootleggers

'The whisky of this country is a most rascally liquor, and by consequence drunk by the most rascally part of the inhabitants', wrote Scotland's national bard, Robbie Burns, in 1788.

In the Highlands illicit whisky was always the toast of defiance and it tasted all the sweeter for being untaxed. Distilling usually took place in the winter months when the region was at its most cut-off. Wisps of smoke would curl into the cold air while an elder of the clan tended the still. Others would be perched on nearby crags straining to catch a glimpse of approaching excisemen, or 'gaugers' out to catch the whisky-makers red handed.

The Government offered a reward of £5 to anyone reporting an illicit still, but this was turned against them. Once the copper 'worm', the most expensive single item of distilling apparatus, wore out, the bootleggers would simply leave it behind, move their dismantled still elsewhere, and claim the reward

More ingenuity was required to get the whisky to market across the Highland Line. One favourite trick was to send a party with some mules and a few casks strapped to their backs in one direction as a decoy. Once the Government troops and excisemen had been lured out of their barracks, the main consignment of whisky could pass unmolested via another route.

One of the most notorious gaugers was Malcolm Gillespie who patrolled the hills around Aberdeen. Armed to the teeth, Gillespie claimed to have impounded 6,535 gallons of whisky, 407 stills, 165 horses and 85 carts during his long reign of terror. Eventually he fell foul of his masters and was arrested for corruption. Not many smugglers wept when he was led to the scaffold to be hung in 1827.

direct form the distillers and blend them up in their cellars. At first these blends were sold locally in stone jars over the counter, but with the advent of the railways and modern bottling lines their reputation began to spread. The real credit however goes to a small band of entrepreneurs who were determined to wean drinkers outside Scotland onto this new vice called whisky. In the 1860's they received help from an unlikely source – a tiny, vine-eating bug called phylloxera that had begun to munch its way through Europe's vineyards and devastated those of Cognac – whisky's great rival.

At the tail end of the Victorian era, demand for blended Scotch was booming. To supply the malt to make the blends, new distilleries began to sprout up everywhere. This first boom was followed by bust and the whisky industry slipped into the 20th century with an almighty hangover. At home sales fell due to rising taxes and then war, while US prohibition closed off a hugely important market, at least in theory. In practice, plenty of Scotch whisky did seep into the States during the 1920's when the country was officially 'dry'.

The most recent chapter in the history of Scotch has been the resurgence of malt whisky led by Glenfiddich in the 1960's. Single malts

*Distillery workers on Islay (c.1880) taking a break after a hard morning's toil. The mound of peat they
are sitting on would have been cut in the spring from the island's ample peat bogs and left to dry for a few months.
The shovels or 'shiels' were for turning the barley on the malt floor.*

The logo on the world's best-selling Scotch whisky depicts a striding man in top hat and tails, and carries the strapline; 'born 1820 and still going strong'. That was the year the original Johnnie Walker inherited money to open a grocery store in his hometown of Kilmarnock, though whether he ever dressed like a Regency dandy seems unlikely. He probably blended tea at first and eventually moved on to blending whisky – an art he taught his son Alexander. It was Alexander who turned 'Walker's Old Highland Whisky' into the world-beating Johnnie Walker brand.

may well have been the original Scotch, but due to the popularity of blends, it seems they had all but disappeared as far as whisky drinkers were concerned. Today single malts are far more than just a blending ingredient and are proudly bottled by almost every malt distillery in Scotland.

WHO INVENTED SCOTCH?

The Scots were doubtless making whisky before the first official mention of 1494, but it remains a mystery as to precisely where or when. One theory is that it all started with the Irish whose monks supposedly brought back the secret of distillation from the Middle East during the Dark Ages. There are tales of Irish chieftains fortifying themselves and their troops with a slug of 'the hard stuff' before battle, and, more recently, an ancient 'worm' – the copper coil used to condense spirit, was found in an Irish bog. The country's early missionaries like St Colomba certainly brought Christianity to Scotland when they arrived in the Western Isles. Though whether they also brought with them the art of making whisky is another matter.

The Whisky Barons

When the Victorian middle-classes discovered whisky on their trips to the Highlands, they found it a bracing outdoor spirit that was fine for the grouse moor or the riverbank, but not really suitable for drinking at home or in their clubs. To persuade them otherwise, it took a dedicated band of Scottish entrepreneurs. Tommy Dewar, the son of a small-time blender in Perth, was a classic example. Starting in 1885, he built Dewars White Label into a world-beating brand with production passing a million gallons by 1900. It is still the biggest-selling blend in America. His arch rival was James Buchanan, who also made millions from his 'Black & White', as did Peter Mackie the man behind 'White Horse'. By the 1920's these whiskies all became part of the mighty Distillers Company (now Diageo), though Dewars has since left the fold to join Bacardi. Also from Perth was 'Famous Grouse', created by a local wine merchant Matthew Gloag, and 'Bells' registered by Arthur Bell in 1896. While in Aberdeen, the family grocery business of Chivas Brothers launched the world-famous Chivas Regal in 1909, now a deluxe 12 year-old blend.

How Scotch is Made

The curious thing about Scotch whisky production is how little it has changed. If Scotland's first distillers could come back from the grave and visit a modern-day malt distillery they would recognise the process if not the scale. A trip to an equivalent grain distillery whose giant column stills resemble an oil refinery, might totally spook them however.

As with any recipe, you have to start by assembling the ingredients, which in the case of malt whisky, are just barley, water and a little yeast. The cold, clear water needed for whisky-making is plentiful in Scotland as is grain from the fertile east coast. There are different strains of barley and some distilleries, notably Macallan, insist they do make a difference to the end result. If true, the differences are subtle and nothing like the effect that different grape varieties have on wine for example.

The barley first has to be malted which was traditionally done in the distillery. The grain was steeped in cold water and then spread on a stone floor in the malt barn to dry and begin germinating. The malt was turned regularly with a

Making malt whisky involves steeping the barley in water and drying it over a kiln. It is then ground in a mill and mixed with hot water to create the mash. This is injected with yeast and left to ferment like beer. Then comes a double distillation in a copper still and a long maturation in oak.

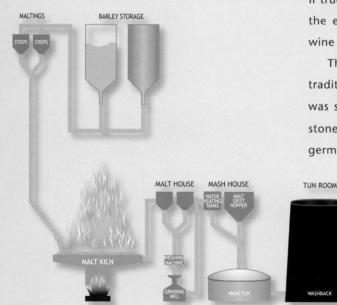

MALTINGS   BARLEY STORAGE

STEEPS STEEPS

MALT HOUSE   MASH HOUSE   TUN ROOM   STILL HOUSE   WAREHOUSE

WATER HEATING TANKS   MALT GRIST HOPPER

CONDENSER

CONDENSER

MALT KILN

WEIGHING MACHINE

GRINDING MILL   MASH TUN   WASHBACK   WASH STILL   SPIRIT STILL   SPIRIT RECEIVER   SPIRIT STORE

In a traditional distillery the barley was malted in-house. After a week spread out on a stone floor it was taken here to the drying floor above the kiln to soak up the peat smoke.

The wash (opposite) in full ferment at Glenfiddich.

they rely on outside maltings like everyone else. These produce malt in large rotating drums and can supply it with a precise level of smokiness – from 'unpeated' to 'heavily peated'.

The malted barley is ground into a coarse porridge and tipped into the mash tun – a large, stainless steel vessel. It acts rather like a coffee percolator using hot water to extract all the goodness, in this case soluble sugars, from the mixture. The resulting sweet, syrupy liquid is injected with yeast as it's pumped into the wash backs – tall, circular vats traditionally made of pine. It is then left to ferment for about 48 hours.

At this point the distillery smells just like a brewery, though the beer produced known as the wash is a murky, unstable brew at 8% alcohol. It is turned into high-strength spirit by being boiled up in a pair of gleaming copper stills. Although all

wooden shovel to prevent it matting and after about a week was laid on a wire mesh above a large kiln. In the Highlands and the Western Isles, the most common form of fuel was peat which was cut from peat bogs in the spring. A brick of peat smells of nothing until it starts to smoulder on the fire. It then impregnates the malt with its dense, blue smoke. The aroma is pungent, but not unpleasant. Today it is the aroma most commonly associated with whiskies from the west coast, particularly from Islay. Only a handful of distilleries like Highland Park, Balvenie and Laphroaig still malt their own barley and even

stills share the same basic shape – a broad, bulbous base with a tall, tapering neck, they do vary from one distillery to the next. This, and how fast the stills are run, dictates the amount of contact there is between the liquid and the copper. And this in turn subtly effects the character of the whisky and helps make each single malt unique.

All Scotch malt whisky is distilled twice to achieve a pure, full-strength spirit. The 'wash still' takes the strength up to a half-way stage and the 'spirits still' finishes the job. It works like all distillation because the component parts of the wash have different boiling points allowing the distiller to separate the 'good' alcohols from the 'bad'. As the spirits still begins to boil, alcoholic vapours rise up the neck and escape through an angled pipe at the top where they are

then condensed back into liquid. To do this some distilleries use a traditional 'worm' or coil suspended in a large tub of cold water, others use a modern condenser.

In both cases the condensed spirit flows through a spout in the spirits safe – a small, padlocked box of glass and polished brass. What flows at first is known as the 'foreshots' and is rejected for being highly alcoholic and full of impurities. As these decline, the stillman gets ready to redirect the spout and save the 'middle cut'. Some impurities will remain but these are

All whisky stills have a bulbous base and a tall neck, and they are always made of copper. The precise design however can vary dramatically from one distillery to the next.

The stillman (opposite) carefully checks the new-make spirit as it flows through the spirits safe.

Second-Hand Barrels

All Scotch whisky is matured in second-hand barrels. This not just the Scots being frugal and wanting to save money, it is because the vanilla flavours of new oak would simply swamp the whisky. Luckily the American whiskey industry are only allowed to use their barrels once to make Bourbon, which means a ready supply of hand-me-down casks for Scotland. Today the vast majority of Scotch is aged in ex-Bourbon barrels, with the rest in ex-Sherry casks from Spain. Occasionally something more exotic is used like a Madeira cask or a Port pipe from Portugal to 'finish' the whisky and give it an added twist.

Maturation is the part of the process most subject to chance. Before the end of distillation, every stage is pre-determined from the level of peat smoke in the malt to the speed of the stills. Suddenly this carefully crafted spirit is tipped into a mixed assortment of barrels and left to suck in flavours from the wood and breath out alcohol. Evaporation, the so-called 'Angel's Share', equates to around 150 million bottles a year. The only consolation is none of them paid any tax!

What the cask previously contained is just one of many variables in maturation. As is the size of the cask, whether it is European or American oak, and how many times it has been used before to age Scotch. A first-fill Sherry cask will have far more influence than a fourth-hand Bourbon barrel. Add in external factors like how cold and damp the warehouse is, and then multiply these together and the variables in maturing Scotch whisky can be infinite.

what give whisky much of its character. Technically they are called 'congeners' and there can be as many as 400 in a good single malt compared to just two in a bottle of vodka. Unfortunately they make for a worse hang-over if you over indulge.

As the strength continues to fall, the so-called 'feints' begin to appear. At first they are sweet-smelling and worth keeping, but as they deteriorate they are rejected and sent to join the foreshots. This is a critical moment and varies from one distillery to the next depending on the type of whisky sought – whether something smooth and gentle or rich and robust.

What flows through the spirits safe to be filled into oak casks is known as 'new make' spirit. It cannot legally be called Scotch until it has been aged for at least three years. It can be fascinating to compare the new make character of the spirit with the final product, bottled perhaps ten or twelve years later. How distant the two are in character is all down to maturation – perhaps the most important and least understood part of the entire process.

Compared to the violent transformation from grain to spirit in the distillery, the time spent maturing in wood appears all quiet and tranquillity. The minute day to day changes are far too small to measure. But multiply them by ten years and the transformation can be every bit as dramatic as distillation. In fact with a single malt aged in an active cask, maturation may account for as much of two thirds of its character.

A warehouseman at Glenlivet rolls a cask into place, in this case a standard 'hogshead' or 'hoggie'
that once contained American Bourbon. Most malt Scotch whisky is matured in such casks, though a fair amount is
aged in Sherry butts. Occasionally something more exotic like a wine barrique or Port pipe is used.

*Strathisla on Speyside is the spiritual home of Chivas Regal. The still room is
the heart of any malt distillery. Come here in the depths of winter when those gleaming copper
stills are radiating warmth and whisky, and you will never want to leave.*

MALT WHISKY REGIONS

Speyside

There are traditionally four main whisky regions in Scotland, each with its own individual style – from the more gentle, floral malts of Speyside, to the rich, robust, smoky whiskies of the west coast. That said, there are always exceptions to the rule.

The River Spey is a beautiful fast-flowing river that clatters its way northwards for over a hundred miles to the Moray Firth in the north east of Scotland. In the area between Grantown and Elgin, you will find the greatest concentration of malt whisky distilleries in the world. The question is why?

Well one answer lies in the area's remoteness. Come here at the start of winter and you can sense Speyside beginning to close in on itself behind the vast, granite bulk of the Cairngorms. In the past, it was far more isolated than now, with many of the higher routes into the region blocked by snow and ice. This gave the early malt distillers the freedom to develop their craft in peace without rules and regulations imposed from outside.

Another clue is obviously the river Spey itself signifying an abundance of cold, crystal clear water – an essential ingredient for making whisky. Perhaps curiously however, most distilleries rely on underground springs and none take their water directly from the Spey. There was also plenty of fuel, initially in the form of peat, to malt the barley and fire the stills, and there was usually just enough local barley. In addition, the early distillers may have had some experience in at least the first part of the process – that of brewing. There was ancient tradition of making heather ale on Speyside.

But perhaps the real reason Speyside has become the largest, most important whisky region in Scotland is down to that simple truth that nothing succeeds like success. By the time the whisky industry went legal in the 1820's, the art of making good whisky was too deeply bred in the bone to disappear. Then again, the old

ISLANDS

SPEYSIDE

HIGHLANDS

LOWLANDS

Like many popular single malts, Glenfiddich comes in a variety of bottlings to complement its standard 12 year-old. These range from older expressions, to cask strength ones, to different cask finishes.

The wrought iron entrance to Cragganmore (opposite) heralds one of the most complex malts on Speyside.

had their own sidings to bring in the grain, fuel and empty barrels, and to take away the filled casks. Not all have survived, but there are still around sixty working distilleries on Speyside.

With so many distilleries in one area, it was probably inevitable that a certain style of malt whisky would evolve here. The whiskies tended to be lightly peated, if at all, and seemed to satisfy the blenders who looked to Speyside to supply the smooth, balanced heart of many of their blends. The best single malts from the region are some of the most complex whiskies you can find. They are all unique, but tend to share a rich, floral, heathery sweetness.

STRATHISLA

With its speckled stone walls like nougat and its twin pagoda roof, Strathisla is as pretty a place for making whisky as you could wish for. It was

benefits of being cut-off suddenly became Speyside's greatest disadvantage. It had to wait for other whisky regions to have their moment of glory. Foremost among these was Campbeltown in the south west. It was closer to the big blenders, particularly those in Glasgow, and for a while became Scotland's great whisky metropolis. But Speyside always had the quality and consistency, and began to grow once it was fully connected by rail to the rest of the country. During the 1890's a rash of new distilleries sprang up beside the old Strathspey line. Many

founded in 1786 in Keith and takes its water from a local well that was once used by brewers in the 11th century making heather ale. It provides the heart of the Chivas Regal blend. And has a delicate, fruitcake character as a single malt.

GLEN GRANT

This solid Victorian distillery was founded by James and John Grant in 1840 and stands just north of the Spey in Rothes. It is particularly popular with visitors from Italy, where Glen Grant 5 year-old is the country's top selling malt. Older expressions have more depth and body with a pleasing dry, nutty finish.

GLENFIDDICH

To meet demand for the biggest selling malt in the world, the still-house at Glenfiddich in Dufftown has no less than 29 stills. With its pale-straw colour and light – medium body, it may not be the last word in complexity, but it has introduced millions to the taste of single malt. For those seeking something more, try one of the older expressions of its stable-mate, made in the ground of Glenfiddich, the sweet, blossom-scented Balvenie.

CRAGGANMORE

John Smith was one of the most experienced distillers on Speyside when he founded Cragganmore in 1869. It stands apart from the main cluster of Speyside distilleries, a little deeper into the Highlands at Ballindalloch. This may explain

Speyburn is a classic Victorian distillery in Rothes on Speyside.

The still room at Glenrothes on Speyside can produce up to 5 million litres of spirits a year. Until recently however, barely a drop of this delicious whisky was bottled as a single malt, such was its demand among blenders.

GLENLIVET

This famous distillery, the first in its glen to go legal and get a licence in 1824, stands aloof from the bustle of Dufftown and Rothes, in a wide, windswept bowl by the braes of Glenlivet. It may have lost some of its prestige over the years, but it is still very popular especially in the USA. Of its main expressions, there is a light, vanilla-scented 12 year-old and the altogether more succulent and flowery 18 year-old.

THE MACALLAN

This old farm distillery was almost certainly supplying whisky on the side well before it gained a licence in 1824. Its original customers would have been drovers, stopping here with their cattle before heading south. Today The Macallan is a highly rated single malt which has long been aged in Sherry casks – hence its distinctive amber colour and resinous Christmas cake flavour.

GLENROTHES

Despite being one of the larger Speyside distilleries with five pairs of stills, Glenrothes was almost unknown until recently. This was because almost everything it produced disappeared into blends, notably Cutty Sark. Today, thanks to its owners having an enlightened change of heart, the best casks are set aside for a deliciously indulgent single malt.

some of its robust, slightly smoky character, or it may have more to do with its uniquely shaped stills. Who knows – either way, this famous 'Classic Malt' is well worth seeking out.

CARDHU

Like many distilleries on Speyside, Cardhu began life on the farm supplying illicit hooch to a largely local clientele. It was licensed in 1824 and by the end of the 19th century, was one of the key malts in Johnnie Walker. The link with the famous blend endures, though there is little to spare these days. Thanks to its popularity in Spain, most goes into a silky smooth 12 year-old malt.

MALT WHISKY REGIONS
The Highlands

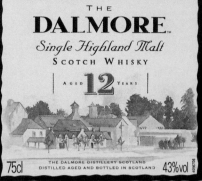

Scotland is split in two as if by an axe. This geological rift is the Highland Boundary Fault which runs north east from the Firth of Clyde to the coast south of Aberdeen, and is clearly visible from space. For much of its history the split was more than just geographical. Put simply the north was a different country to the more populated, prosperous south. While farming and industry rapidly transformed in the Lowlands, changes came more slowly to the Highlands, and for some time, life carried on pretty much as it always had.

This affected everything including the making of whisky which was arguably more important here than anywhere else. Even now the thought of enduring a long Highland winter without the warmth and solace of good whisky is hard to imagine. Back then it

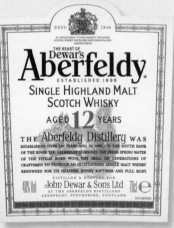

was almost a psychological necessity. Distilling became part of the calendar, an activity that followed on naturally from the harvest and was finished well before spring. It became woven into the culture as much as Highland dress and music.

The more enlightened law-makers of the 18th century recognised these differences. They also made allowances for the low yields compared to the more fertile Lowlands, by imposing less duty on those who owned a still so long as they didn't try and sell their whisky outside the region. The trouble was, many distillers found life beyond the law more attractive. It meant paying no tax at all, and being able to supply smuggled whisky to an appreciative audience in the south who recognised its quality.

Two malts showing the diversity of the Highlands – Dalmore from the banks of the Cromarty Firth is a dark sumptuous whisky compared to the minty, vanilla-scented malt of Aberfeldy, made in the undulating hills of the Tay valley beyond Perth.

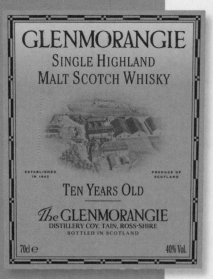

After 1830 most of the big, Lowland distilleries turned to making grain whisky using the new continuous stills. From then on, the Highlands became the true home of malt whisky. Whether there has ever been a definitive style from the region is another matter however. Being such a vast area that stretches from the fringes of Glasgow to the very tip of northern Scotland, you would think not, especially since most individual distillers operated in isolation, supplying their whisky locally. And yet people in the whisky business still talk of 'Highland' malt as distinct from other regions.

On the whole they mean a whisky that is more robust than Lowland and usually with less heather honey sweetness than Speyside. Highland whisky is often quite smoky, though not as pungent as malts from the Western Isles. In addition coastal distilleries like Old Pulteney in Wick and Oban on the West Coast, often share a slightly salty tang. This maritime flavour contrasts with the softer, more fruity style you might find in Perthshire with a malt like Aberfeldy.

HIGHLAND PARK

This famous distillery on Orkney is as far-flung as you could wish for, but definitely worth visiting for those who make the crossing to the island by plane or ferry.

The Congregation of Highland Park

The most famous legend about Highland Park is that this was the site where Magnus Eunson carried out his trade as the most notorious smuggler on Orkney. By day he was a Presbyterian minister, but by night he was a distiller of illicit hooch that he used to keep in a cask stashed under his pulpit. It was by keeping his ear to the ground that he got wind that the excise officers were finally planning a raid on his church. Quickly the barrels were assembled in the aisle and the lid of a coffin placed on top, over which was thrown a white sheet. When the excisemen burst in, the assembled crowd, led by Eunson, let up a great wail for the dead. All that was needed was for one of the congregation to whisper the dreaded word 'smallpox', the anthrax of its day, and the officer and his men turned and fled.

Highland Park was founded in 1798 by Magnus Eunson, a notorious smuggler whose day job as a Presbyterian minister gave him the perfect cover. As a complex, well-balanced 12 year-old, it has traces of smoke, spice and a heathery sweetness.

OLD PULTENEY

Established in 1826 in Wick, just south of John O'Groats, Old Pulteney had a captive audience right on its doorstep. Wick was a booming fishing port whose inhabitants had an almost insatiable thirst for whisky until the town voted to go 'dry' in 1922. Somehow the distillery survived and today produces a clean, refreshing, faintly aromatic single malt.

GLENMORANGIE

Moving down the east coast to the Dornoch Firth you will find Glenmorangie whose tall, elegant stills are working flat out these days. The result is a charming, gentle whisky with a slight scent of orange peel and smoke. It is available in a range of different cask finishes and claims to be Scotland's most popular single malt.

DALMORE

This distillery on the banks of the Cromarty Firth was established in 1839. With so much of its production disappearing into blends, notably Whyte & Mackay, it is not so well-known as a single malt. This is a shame – as it is sumptuous, slightly spicy whisky with a similar, though more obvious candied fruit aroma than Glenmorangie.

Highland Park is classic, rather cramped Victorian distillery on Orkney. It has long promoted itself as the most northerly distillery in Britain. This may have to be revised if plans to build a small, boutique distillery on Shetland go ahead.

23

Edradour, near Pitlochry in Perthshire is a classic farm distillery that has not really evolved. At one time most distilleries would have looked like this, but today it feels distinctly pocket-sized, producing in a year what a typical Speyside distillery produces in a week.

EDRADOUR

If you wish to get back to the small-scale, artisan roots of whisky-making in the Highlands, you cannot do better than Edradour – a tiny, doll's-house distillery in the rolling hills beyond Pitlochry. In fact, because so little is made, your best chance of trying this minty, luscious malt is to visit the distillery itself.

ABERFELDY

The role of this Perthshire distillery, built at the height of the late Victorian whisky boom, is obvious the moment you arrive. Aberfeldy exists to provide the heart and soul of Dewar's – the most popular blend of Scotch in America. You get the full brand experience in the visitor's centre, after which you can sample a drop of this delicate, vanilla-scented malt.

DALWHINNIE

Driving north up the A9, the main road to the Highlands, you are well into the mountains before you reach the Drumochter Pass and Dalwhinnie – Scotland's highest distillery. At just over 1000 feet, the weather here can be cold and bleak in the extreme, in other words – perfect for making whisky. After 15 years in the cask, Dalwhinnie is bottled as a 'Classic Malt' with a smooth, honeyed flavour and smoky fragrance.

OBAN

Oban was a tiny fishing village when Hugh Stevenson built his distillery here in 1794. Since then, the port has expanded considerably into what is now 'the gateway to the Western Isles', rather dwarfing the distillery in the process. With just two stills producing a fresh, lightly peat-smoked malt, it must work hard to meet the demand as one of the 'Classic Malts'.

MALT WHISKY REGIONS

The Islands

The islands that form a necklace round the west coast of Scotland are pretty easy to visit these days. Most of the larger ones have regular ferry sailings to the mainland and one or two even have airports – albeit on a small scale. The beach landing strip on Tiree is hardly London Heathrow. Yet flights and ferry crossings do get cancelled because of the weather, and if you are caught in the midst of a bad winter storm, you can become stranded for a while. Such occasions give some inkling of just how isolated most of these islands were for much of their history.

This isolation bred a real island mentality for making do with whatever was to hand. To survive, the islands had to be self-sufficient, though it was never easy. There was usually enough rough grazing for sheep, but the ground was often poor and crops were hard to grow and easily flattened by gale-force winds. Yet most islands grew a little grain and some of this would be turned into whisky.

Travellers to the Western Isles had long been fascinated by all aspects of island life, including how much people drank. As one visitor to the Outer Hebrides noted in the 1780's '...of every year's production of Barley, a third or fourth part is distilled into a spirit called whisky, of which the natives are immoderately fond'. Another mentioned the custom of how the elders of the clan would sit in a circle for up to two days and sup whisky from a shell that would be passed round at regular intervals. Those who collapsed would be carried away in a wheel-barrow until the gathering finally broke up.

Small-scale distilling became wide-spread, encouraged by the growing number of people on the islands and the freedom to operate outside the law. On Tiree it was said that every farmer operated at least one still, almost all of them illegally. In the whole of the

Bowmore, the oldest distillery on Islay, is now owned by the giant Japanese drinks company Suntory. It was established in 1779 and produces a characteristically smoky malt, though less pungent than those on the south coast of the island like Laphroaig and Ardbeg.

BOWMORE
ISLAY
SINGLE MALT
SCOTCH WHISKY

BOWMORE DISTILLERY

AGED **12** YEARS

700 ml e   DISTILLED AND BOTTLED IN SCOTLAND   40% Vol.

LAGAVULIN

After a period of working a three day week, this legendary distillery on Islay now works flat out to quench a world-wide thirst for its single malt. But patience is required, for it takes 16 years in cask before Lagavulin is considered ready for bottling.

unlikely to produce a soft, understated whisky as though it were nestled among rolling hills in the Lowlands.

The style of whisky was appreciated by the blenders, but only as a top dressing to add spice and character to their blends. Not much was required in other words, and this, together with their physical remoteness, made life very hard for island distillers. Those that survived have been saved by the recent surge in interest in single malts.

TALISKER

When Skye's famous distillery was founded in 1830, there were seven licensed distilleries on this island off Scotland's north-west coast. Now there is only Talisker which still feels remote, staring out to sea behind the dark, volcanic peaks of the Cuillin Hills. There is something almost volcanic about the whisky, which slowly erupts on the tongue with a fiery, peppery intensity.

THE ISLAND OF ISLAY

If the Irish really did introduce the Scots to whisky as they like to claim, it was presumably via somewhere like Islay, that is only twenty miles from the tip of Northern Ireland. As the most fertile island in the Hebrides, there was

Hebrides, excluding Islay, there were only 13 distilleries ever licensed. Yet during the 19th century whisky-making on the islands started to follow what was happening in the rest of Scotland. Most of the smaller distilleries disappeared, while a few larger ones survived to supply the blenders on the mainland. The style of whisky was almost invariably pungent and full of fire and smoke. This simply reflected the harsh environment of life on the islands. A storm-tossed distillery like Talisker on the Isle of Skye was usually enough grain to make whisky, though in poor years there was always a debate whether it should be saved for food. There was also no shortage of water and abundant peat bogs which provided the island's only source of fuel.

The smell of peat smoke would have impregnated everything from people's hair and clothing, to the walls of their homes and the food that they ate. Inevitably the whisky they made carried the same flavour. Whether we would like it today is hard to say. It would have been pungent in the extreme, and if it didn't literally put hairs on your chest, it would certainly be an acquired taste. Over the years, the whiskies have been tamed to allow their full complexity and character to shine through.

Unlike the grain which is shipped in from the mainland, the peat is still all home-grown and used to malt the barley at Port Ellen. Islay peat is special, with a faintly sweet fragrance and a pronounced salty, briny character. It has a high moss content which helps soak up the sea air as it

blows in off the Atlantic. These flavours are then infused into the malt to reappear much later in the glass when the whisky is fully matured. This can be a slow process for a heavily smoked whisky like Lagavulin which spends sixteen years in wood before it is bottled.

Today there are seven working distilleries on this relatively small island of 3500 people. Strength in numbers and a long tradition in the art of whisky-making has been part of the success. But just as important has been the strong sense of

Ardbeg has become increasingly popular as a single malt. It shares the same peat-smoked richness as its near neighbours, Lagavulin and Laphroaig. Being right on the water's edge, its whisky seems to soak up the salty, maritime aroma of the sea.

Laphroaig's gentle setting at dusk belies the fiery intensity of its single malt, with its peaty, medicinal flavour. According to legend, it was this note that allowed the whisky to be sold as a surgical spirit to Americans during US Prohibition in the 1920's.

identity. While Islay whiskies all differ they share some-thing of the house style, characterised by the strange, bitter-sweet aroma of Islay peat. It is a taste that many malt whisky drinkers have grown to love.

BOWMORE

The little town of Bowmore, Islay's capital, barely existed when its distillery was founded in 1779. Today it is the oldest licensed distillery on the west coast, and still retains its traditional floor maltings and peat-fired kiln to produce a medium-peated, aromatic whisky with a dry, smoky finish.

BRUICHLADDICH

If few people outside the whisky industry had heard of Islay's Bruichladdich it was understandable – most of what it produced disappeared into blends. This changed in 2000 when an independent company rescued the distillery which had been closed for five years. A dry, moder-ately smoky malt in a whole raft of different ages is now produced.

LAGAVULIN

This famous 'Classic Malt' is produced on the south coast of Islay in a distillery that merged out of a number of smuggling bothies to go legal in 1817. In summer, when the sea is calm, it is a bucolic, gentle spot, but don't let that fool you. Lagavulin is a rich, full-bodied, smoke-scented monster of a malt.

LAPHROAIG

There is nothing shy or retiring about Lagavulin's neighbour either. Equally picturesque, yet equally big and bold. The distillery was founded in 1815 and is one of the few to still malt its own barley. The result is an intense, maritime whisky, infused with the taste of sea-spray and seaweed and a dry, slightly bitter finish.

ARDBEG

Completing the trio of distilleries on the south coast of Islay, is Ardbeg, which in some expressions may be the most heavily peat-smoked of them all. Somehow to enjoy this dense, gloriously tangy single malt at its best, you need to come here and drink it outdoors, preferably with a storm brewing out at sea.

MALT WHISKY REGIONS

The Lowlands

The regional nature of malt whisky is down to history if nothing else. Distilleries did not grow up thinking to sell their whiskies all round the world as many of them do today. They almost invariably started on a small scale with limited horizons producing a whisky that reflected its environment and which would appeal locally. Having created a style that was popular, there was no incentive to change it as demand spread. The whisky industry is innately conservative.

Although malt whisky became very much associated with the Highlands and Islands there were once over 200 licensed malt distilleries in the Lowlands. Quite why there are now only two in production is not entirely clear. They were reigned in by the law much sooner than their cousins in the north and no doubt the need to compete with them and pay taxes must have felt unfair.

Maybe the real reason is that malt whisky feeds off the romantic image of Scotland which is inextricably bound up with the Highlands.

Without that backdrop of heather-clad hills, misty mountains and the sound of water chuckling in the burn, Lowland distilleries will somehow always be in the shade.

GLENKINCHIE

This red brick distillery, a short drive south of Edinburgh produces a dry, aperitif-style malt. It is surrounded by fields of grain, and in keeping with its surroundings Glenkinchie produces a light, straw-coloured malt with the aroma of cut grass.

AUCHENTOSHAN

Glasgow's closest distillery at Dalmuir was founded in 1823 beside the Clyde on the site of an ancient monastery. Auchentoshan shares that unpeated, malty flavour of Glenkinchie though is perhaps even smoother thanks to its Irish-style triple distillation. It has a light straw colour and a delicate, cereal flavour.

The Lowlands used to boast many distilleries at one time, but today there are only two in commercial production on either side of the country – Glenkinchie, south of Edinburgh and Auchentoshan beside the Clyde.

The Whisky Scene

Once wartime restrictions on distilling in Scotland were lifted after World War II, Scotch enjoyed a golden period. In established export markets like the USA, it reigned supreme, while vodka remained a distant glimmer in the rear-view mirror. At the same time new markets were opening up. From Venezuela to Japan, people were turning their back on the home-grown spirits drunk by their parents in favour of Scotch. Big brands like Chivas Regal, Johnnie Walker and Ballantine's were advertised everywhere as something glamourous to aspire to.

Production increased year by year until the whisky loch was full to overflowing. By 1975 over one billion gallons of whisky lay in warehouses round Scotland. In fairness to the distillers, trying to guess future demand has always been incredibly difficult. While the weathermen have trouble predicting tomorrow's weather, every distillery has to forecast how thirsty people will be in several years to come.

In the early eighties whisky went through a painful contraction with many distilleries being 'mothballed' or closed for good. Part of the problem was declining sales back home where Scotch did not have the added cachet of being an imported luxury. All too often it was 'what the

A superior collection of malts from Chivas Brothers.

old man drank' and therefore terminally 'uncool' to a younger generation attracted to the latest, brightly packaged brand of vodka.

Annual whisky consumption in Britain peaked at around 4 bottles a head in 1979. Since when it has declined to between 2 – 3 bottles. Like all spirits it has been heavily taxed from one Budget to the next. At the time of writing the duty on Scotch was £5.48 a bottle – a level it has stood at for a number of years. When you take off the VAT from the final price of a basic blend, there is often not much left. The picture is of course different for single malts which have become evermore popular.

Scotland's national drink remains a huge global force with over nine out of ten bottles drunk overseas. You only have to watch a young crowd drinking whisky, often mixed with Coke, late into the night in trendy bars in Barcelona or Athens, to realise its image is often higher than it is back home. A decade into the new millennium, and Scotch is on a roll once more thanks to surging demand in countries like China. Maybe it will be a while before a billion Chinese toast in their New Year with a dram, but the industry is full of confidence. In 2007, Britain's biggest distiller, unveiled plans for a massive new £40 million distillery on Speyside. It won't be the last.

TWO STORIES

Five Minutes' Peace
and All in One Piece

JILL MURPHY